This adventure belongs to

_____ .

I,_____, *will do my best*
to obey the golden rule of travel.

Anywhere Once

The Essential Self-Guided Travel Journal for

Paris, France

Travel Should
Be An Adventure—
Let's Map It Together

Tani Lamb

Lamb Chop Publishing
11700 Preston Rd Ste 660
#678
Dallas, Texas 75230
www.anywhereonce.com

The information provided in this travel journal is for general informational purposes only. While we strive to provide accurate and up-to-date information, we make no representations or warranties of any kind, express or implied, about the completeness, accuracy, reliability, suitability, or availability with respect to the journal or the information, products, services, or tourist attractions contained in the journal for any purpose. Therefore, any reliance on such information is strictly at your own risk.

ISBN: 979-8-9912061-0-5 - Paperback
ISBN: 979-8-9912061-1-2 - Hardcover

LCCN: 2024922820

Printed in the United States of America

♾ This paper meets the requirements of ANSI/NISO Z39.48-1992 (Permanence of Paper)

Cover Art: Pierre Mercieca

1 1 1 9 2 4

Dedicated to
Bishop Willie Lamb

"And when I passed by thee, and saw thee polluted in thine own blood, I said unto thee when thou wast in thy blood, Live; yea, I said unto thee when thou wast in thy blood, Live."
Ezekiel 16:6

CONTENTS

The Golden Rule of Travel   1

Before Your Trip—*Avant Votre Voyage*   2

What is Your Number?—*Quel est vôtre numéro?*   6

The Museums—*Les Musées*   8

Art Bonus—*Bonus Artistique*   24

The Attractions—*Les Attractions*   26

Where to Eat—*Où Manger*   30

The Food—*La Cuisine*   32
  Crêpes & Galettes   32
  The Cheeses—*Les Fromages*   34
  The Sandwiches—*Les Sandwiches*   36
  Some Like It Hot! Hot Chocolate—
        Le Chocolat Chaud   38
  You Do Not Have to Dress up to
        Enjoy the Opéra   40
  Duck, Duck, Goose!—
        Canard, Canard, Oie!   42
  It's a Slow Dish but a Great Meal Starter...
        Let's Go, Escargot!   44
  You Knead to Try the Bread—
        Les Croissants   46
        Les Baguettes   48
  Macarons—My Sweet Spot   50
  Onion Soup   52

Your Souvenirs—*Vos Souvenirs*   54

After Your Trip—*Après Votre Voyage*   56
  The Artist—*L'artiste*   57
  The Writer—*L'écrivain*   68

THE GOLDEN RULE OF TRAVEL

Travel often, journey far, and take nothing but memories, souvenirs, and photos.

This travel journal is your keepsake for your personalized adventure in Paris, France. The diary will be divided into two parts. The first part is meant to be done before your trip. It is perfectly fine if you are not planning to go right away. The more research and preparation you do in advance, the better the outcome of your trip. You will then have all the information needed when you land at Charles de Gaulle or Orly Airport, and you can *hit the ground running*. The second part of the journal is to recap your memories while traveling so you will have a written record in addition to your pictures and videos.

BEFORE YOUR TRIP
~*Avant Votre Voyage*

Let's get ready to explore
The City of Light and Love!

France is a country in Europe known for love, chocolate, cheese, museums, fashion, art, and revolution. Paris is the capital, and the residents are called Parisians. The official language of France is French, and the currency used is the euro (€).

What information do you already know about Paris?

_____

_____

_____

What is it about France that has sparked
your interest and made you want to visit?

_____

_____

_____

Which Parisian attraction are you the most excited to see?

_____

_____

_____

Why do you want to visit these attractions?

_____

_____

_____

Have you ever ridden on the subway before?

_____

_____

_____

Do you know about the Paris Metro?

_____

_____

_____

Do you know any French?

If you do not know any French words or phrases, I suggest you learn a few before your trip. Paris is an international city and people working in hotels, restaurants, retail shops, and tourist attractions, can speak multiple languages including English. Parisians that you encounter on the street may only speak French because that is the language spoken in France. It is a polite gesture to attempt to learn a few greetings. Here is a word list that could come in handy. Write the French translation in the column to the right of the word. In the last column, write a shortcut or phonetic sounds you already know or a trick to help you remember the pronunciation.

English	French	Pronunciation
Yes	Oui	We
No	Non	
Hello		
Thank You		
Do You Speak English?		
Please		
I Need Help		
Can You Help Me?		
Good Morning		
Good Night		
Good Evening		

English	French	Pronunciation
Good Afternoon		
That Was Delicious!		
Where is The Restroom?		
One		
Two		
Three		
Four		
Five		
Six		
Seven		
Eight		
Nine		
Ten		
Water		
Water With No Bubbles		
Water With Bubbles		
Juice		
Orange Juice		
Apple Juice		

What Is Your Number?
~*Quel est vôtre numéro?*

Neighborhoods in Paris are called
arrondissements.

There are twenty arrondissements in Paris, and in the place of names, they have numbers. Each arrondissement has its own character and is unique.

Which arrondissement is your favorite?

_____

_____

_____

What famous attractions are there?

_____

_____

Do you know the arrondissement numbers for your favorite attractions?

_____

_____

_____

In which arrondissement is your hotel?

_____

_____

Are there any famous attractions near your hotel?

_____

_____

_____

Is your hotel's arrondissement close to the attractions that you want to see? If so, how far is the walk?

_____

_____

_____

Would you like to consider adding these fascinating attractions near your hotel to your bucket list?

_____

_____

_____

In my second children's book, *The Princess of Sapphires and Sand*, a famous obelisk is located in the Place de la Concorde in **the eighth arrondissement** of Paris, France.

Do you know what an obelisk is?

_____

_____

_____

Would you be interested in taking a photo of this attraction?

_____

_____

_____

THE MUSEUMS
~ *Les Musées*

Paris is world famous for its museums. I have made a list for you.

- *The Cité des Sciences (Science & Industry Museum)*
- *The Paris Natural History Museum & Zoo at the Jardin des Plantes*
- *The Musée Grevin (Wax Museum)*
- *The Louvre Family-Friendly Tours & Experiences*
- *Musée des Arts et Métiers (Museum of Arts and Crafts)*
- *Musée des Arts Forains (Fairground Art Museum)*
- *Le Palais de la découverte (Discovery Palace)*
- *Le Musée des Arts et Métiers (Art and Design Museum)*
- *Le Musée du Quai Branly—Jacques Chirac*
- *Le Musée de l'Armée (Army Museum)*
- *Le Musée de la Magie (Museum of Magic)*
- *Le Musée d'Histoire Naturelle (Museum of Natural History)*
- *Musée d'Orsay (Orsay Museum)*

Do you know these museums?

As you research each museum, write down key points that intrigue you. This way, you will be prepared for your visit and will understand the art and history that awaits you.

The Cité des Sciences
(Science & Industry Museum)

The Paris Natural History Museum & Zoo at the Jardin des Plantes

The Musée Grévin
(Wax Museum)

The Louvre Family-Friendly Tours & Experiences

Musée des Arts et Métiers
(Museum of Arts and Crafts)

Musée des Arts Forains
(Fairground Art Museum)

Le Palais de la découverte
(Discovery Palace)

Le Musée des Arts et Métiers
(Art and Design Museum)

Le Musée du Quai Branly—
Jacques Chirac

Le Musée de l'Armée
(Army Museum)

Le Musée de la Magie
(Museum of Magic)

Le Musée d'Histoire Naturelle
(Museum of Natural History)

Musée d'Orsay
(Orsay Museum)

If you answer a few more questions, it will help tailor your itinerary for your visit.

Did I miss any museums?

_____

_____

_____

*As you delve into the world of Parisian art and culture,
which museums do you feel a connection to? Why?*

_____

_____

*Do you have a favorite artist, sculpturer, or painter?
Which country are they from?*

_____

_____

_____

*What artwork would you like to see at these museums?
Make your list here.*

_____

_____

_____

*In which arrondissement are the museums you would like
to visit?*

_____

_____

*Are your favorite museums open every day? What are the
hours?*

_____

_____

ART BONUS
~ Bonus Artistique

Do you love art?

_____

_____

_____

Are you an artist? Do you enjoy
painting, drawing, or sketching?

_____

_____

_____

Are you familiar with Claude Monet, Edgar Degas,
Camille Pissarro, Auguste Renoir, or Berthe Morisot?
These artists were part of the impressionist movement.

_____

_____

_____

*If you are unfamiliar with these artists,
you can do a little research to see their artwork.
Did you like any of the art that you found?*

_____

_____

_____

*Can you list the artwork you would
like to see from these artists? Would you like
to submerge yourself into the world of Impressionism?*

_____

_____

_____

*If your answer is yes, Musée
d'Orsay is the museum for you.*

The Attractions
~Les Attractions

Have you seen the *Seine River*?

Cruises are offered on the Seine, and if you cruise at night, you can see the Eiffel Tower lit up.

Would you like to add this activity to your list?

_____

_____

_____

*Are there activities you would like
to do on the rivers of Paris other than a cruise?*

_____

_____

_____

The Seine River is about 483 miles long and flows through Paris. This is the second-longest river in France.

Take a guess—how many bridges does the Seine flow under?

Write your answer here!

Okay, enough of the river talk. Let's explore a little dry land. I have created a list of some of the attractions in Paris.

Do you know the attractions below?

I have left space beneath the attraction for you to add your research. After you have gathered your information, you can select a *yes* or *no* option

Montmartre   oui *(yes)* ou *(or)* non *(no)*

Sacré-Cœur   oui ou non

Tuileries Garden   oui ou non

Notre-Dame   oui ou non

Eiffel Tower   oui ou non

Arc de Triomphe   oui ou non

The Conciergerie—
Île de la Cité Marie Antoinette   oui ou non

Luxembourg Garden—
Le Jardin du Luxembourg   oui ou non

Catacombs of Paris   oui ou non

Pompidou Centre—
Place Georges-Pompidou   oui ou non

Champs-Élysées   oui ou non

Are there any amusement parks you would like to see in Paris?

_____

_____

_____

Did I miss an attraction? You can list it here.

| |
| |
| |
| |
| |
| |

WHERE TO EAT
~Où Manger

When you arrive in Paris, you will see a variety of eating establishments. I will list a few of the most common below and fill in the first two. If you know what types of food the others serve, you can fill in the description. If unsure, you can research and then fill in the blank space.

Pâtisserie: French pastry shop that specializes in sweets and desserts.

Michelin Star: The legacy began in 1900, in France, helping French drivers plan their road trips. Now, 124 years later, three Michelin Stars is one of the highest honors awarded to a restaurant for superior cooking. In 2023, Paris had the second-highest number of Michelin-star restaurants in the world.

Brasserie:

_____

_____

_____

Bistro:

_____

_____

_____

Restaurant:

_____

_____

_____

Café:

_____

_____

_____

THE FOOD

~La Cuisine

Paris is known for its food. There are many famous dishes and something for everyone's taste buds. I will name a few foods that I think you may like. If you do not like them, it is okay. You can just write why you do not want to try the dish or cannot wait to indulge.

Crêpe & Galettes

Crêpe

A crêpe is a very thin pancake filled with sweet treats such as fruits and hazelnut spread and then rolled up.

Galette

Galettes are the savory or salty cousins of the sugary crêpe. Galettes are typically filled with meats, cheeses, and vegetables. Many French people eat the fruity crêpe as a dessert, and galettes are usually the main course.

Do you want to try a savory galette? If so, what fillings would you like inside?

_____

_____

_____

Do you know the French translation for your tasty ingredients? Can you say, recognize, or read those meats, vegetables, or cheeses in French? If not, write the French translations here so you can identify them on the menu later.

English	French	Pronunciation

Now, also write the fruits and sweets fillings that you would like in your crêpe here. You can write them in English with the French translation next to it.

English	French	Pronunciation

The Cheeses
~Les Fromages

Now, it is time for things to get a little moldy, blue, and creamy. Trust me, these characteristics are not bad. Do you like cheese? What about Parisian cheeses?

Here are a few delicious options you can find around the capital city.

Chèvre

Comté

Camembert

Roquefort-Blue Cheese

Emmenthal Brie de Meaux

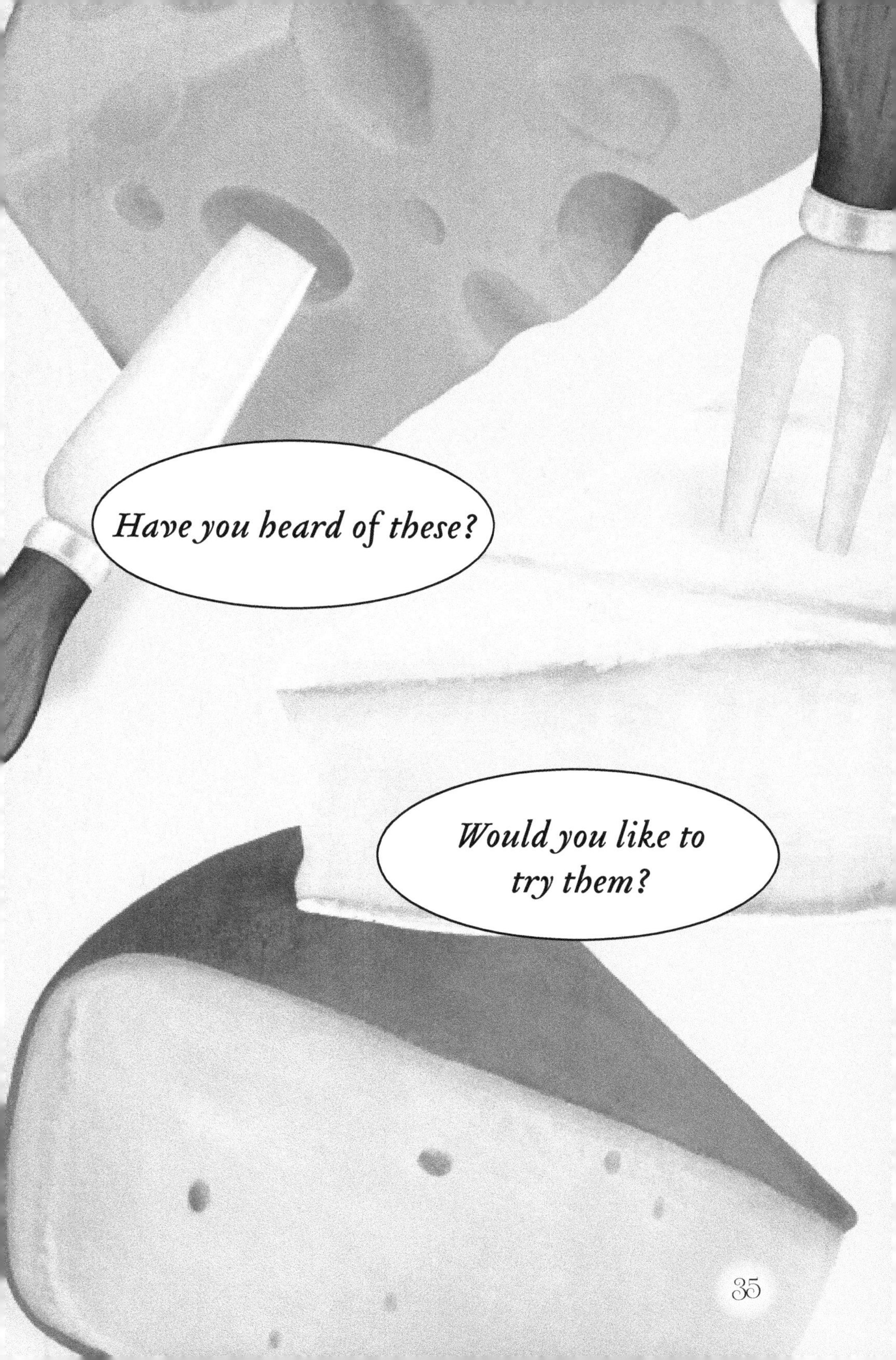
Have you heard of these?
Would you like to try them?

The Sandwiches
~Les Sandwiches

Have you heard of a Croque Monsieur or Croque Madame? They are the Mr. and Mrs. Crunchy ham and cheese sandwiches. What makes them crunchy? Cheese is on the inside and outside, too. This French cheesiness was created in Paris about a hundred years ago. The difference between the sandwiches is an egg. The Croque Madame has an egg on top.

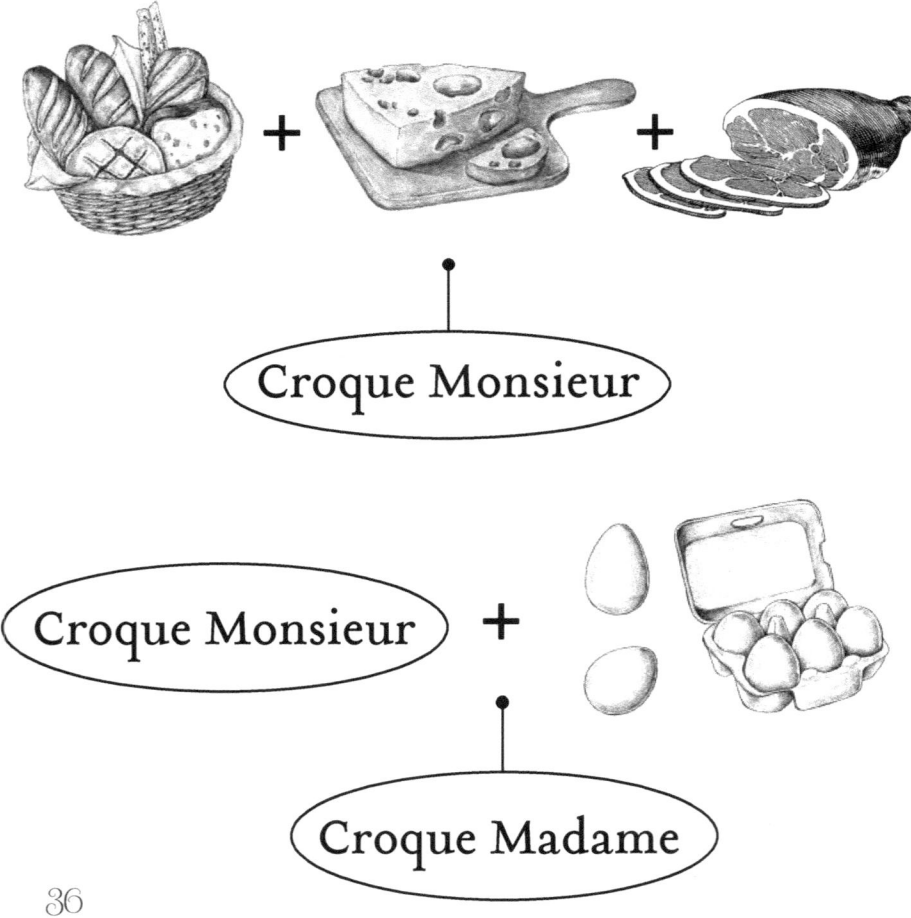

If cheese is not your thing, there is another sandwich. A Jambon-beurre is a French ham sandwich. A fresh baguette is sliced and spread with salty butter, and then filled with thin slices of ham.

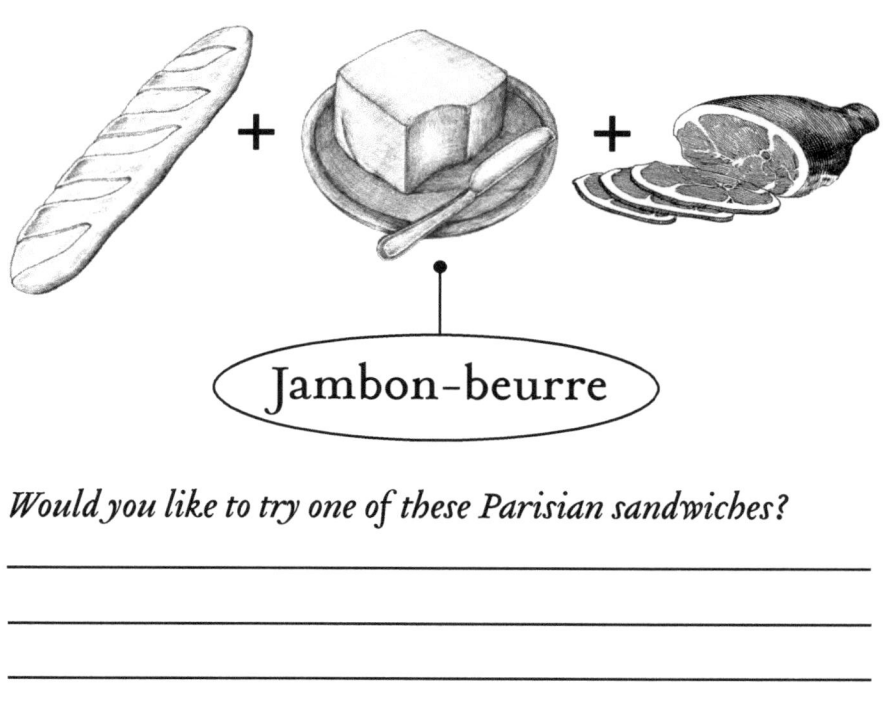

Jambon-beurre

Would you like to try one of these Parisian sandwiches?

_____

_____

_____

Which of these mouthwatering Parisian sandwiches is calling your name? The Mr. or Mrs. Crunchy? Or perhaps the classic, less cheesy Jambon-beurre? Write your choice below.

_____

_____

_____

Some Like It Hot!
Hot Chocolate
~Le Chocolat Chaud

Chocolat chaud, or French-style hot chocolate, is a slowly cooked hot chocolate made with heavy cream, milk, and rich dark cocoa. The delightful drink is moderately sweet. You can add more sugar if desired. One cool thing about this chocolate drink is that it is so rich and creamy that it can support the weight of your spoon. Just place your spoon on top and give it a try. If the chocolatey dessert is made correctly, it should not sink.

Do you want to try a chocolat chaud?

_____

_____

_____

Would you try a French-style hot chocolate in the summer?

_____

_____

_____

You Do Not Have to Dress Up to Enjoy the Opéra

How did the Opera cake receive that name? The origin story of the Opera cake begins with a Parisian pastry chef creating a cake made of consistent layers of coffee-flavored cream, coffee ganache, almond sponge, and chocolate topping. His wife saw this perfectly assembled dessert, and she compared it to the stage of the Paris Opera House.

Another name for the almond-flavored sponge is the Mona Lisa Sponge.

Have you heard of an Opera Cake?

_____

_____

_____

Would you like to try a slice?

_____

_____

_____

Duck, Duck, Goose!
~Canard, Canard, Oie!

People in France are the second largest consumers of duck and goose meat.

Have you ever eaten duck before? What about goose?

_____

_____

_____

Have you heard of any of these popular dishes below?

Foie gras?

Confit de canard?

Canard à l'orange?

Salade Landaise?

Magret De Canard?

It's a Slow Dish but a Great Meal Starter . . . Let's Go, Escargot!

Did you know that snails are mollusks, and when eaten, they are considered seafood? Do you know what a mollusk is? If not, take a second to find the definition and write it here.

_____

_____

_____

Escargot is considered a delicacy in France and is mainly eaten during the Christmas holiday season.

The mollusks are cleaned by boiling them for a short time. They are then removed from their shells, seasoned with herbs, and cooked in oil, wine, or butter.

Would you like to try escargots in France?

_____

_____

_____

You Knead to Try the Bread
~Les Croissants

I enjoy a delicious origin story and will share one with you about croissants and baguettes. These two types of bread were brought to Paris by Viennese bakers. Viennese are people from Vienna, Austria—another European country. German is the language spoken in Austria, and citizens of Austria are called Austrians.

Austrian bakeries opened in Paris in the 1830s, and they sold their tasty buttery croissants. The Viennese pasty evolved, and the croissant, which is light, buttery, shiny, and golden brown, was invented.

Do you like croissants?

_____

_____

_____

Do you think croissants will taste different in France since this is the country that helped the pastry grow in popularity around the world?

_____

_____

_____

So, what do you get if you use the same pastry dough for croissants and add chocolate? You would have the mouth-watering pain au chocolat.

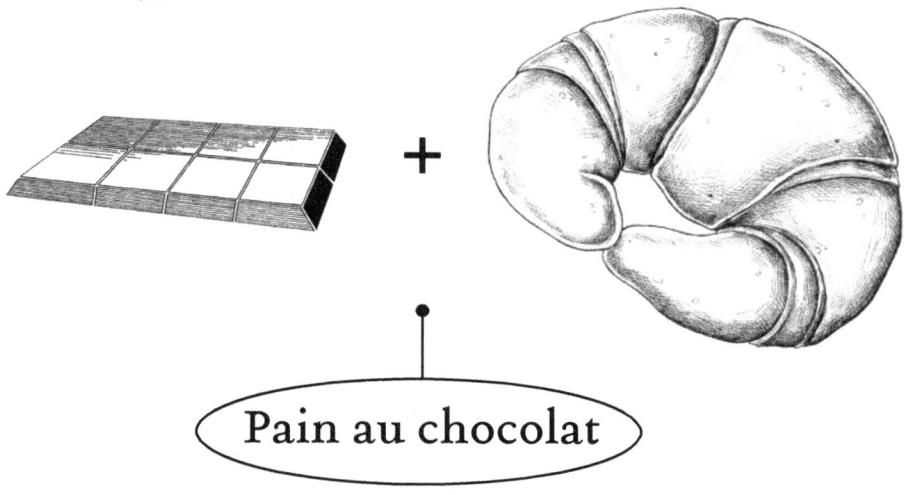

Pain au chocolat

Have you heard of this chocolatey dessert?
Are you going to add it to your food list?

_____

_____

_____

Do you know about the new cookie
croissant invented in Paris? Would you try it?

_____

_____

_____

You Knead to Try the Bread
~Les Baguettes

The baguette was founded in Paris by an Austrian baker in the 1830s. They can be enjoyed solo, as a sandwich, or with a condiment of your choosing. There is more than one way to eat the baguette, and all are correct. The French baguette is flaky and crusty on the outside, and soft and chewy on the inside. These simple yet delicious pieces of perfection are baked daily by artisan bakers.

Have you tried a baguette before?

_____

_____

_____

Do you like baguettes?

_____

_____

_____

Macarons—My Sweet Spot

The Parisian macaron is a round and scrumptious piece of heaven. The crispy shells are made from almond flour and filled with various flavored fillings. This perfectly round sandwich cookie is perfect for a snack or dessert.

Color Me!

A patisserie is a French pastry shop that specializes in sweets and desserts.

Do you know any well-known patisserie houses in France that are famous for their macarons?

_____

_____

_____

Do you want to try macarons in Paris?

oui *(yes)* ou *(or)* non *(no)*

Onion Soup

The French invented onion soup, which dates back to the 1700s or eighteenth century. Onions are inexpensive and tasty, and onion soup is easy to make. You simply caramelize onions and add them to a seasoned broth. When the soup is cooked, you add toasted bread, topped with grated, melted cheese. You can find onion soup in many of the nicer brasseries.

Would you like to try a bowl of Onion Soup?

_____

_____

_____

Are there any other foods you would like to try?
Place them on your list below.

Food List	French

Your Souvenirs
~*Vos Souvenirs*

You can purchase many souvenirs and items that will help you remember your vacation from the City of Light and Love.

How would you like to remember your trip? Would you like a personal portrait from a street sketch artist? What about a beret or scarf?

_____

_____

_____

If you are unsure, here are a few more suggestions: a French cookbook for children, postcards for a scrapbook, a mini figurine of one of the iconic structures, keyrings, or magnets. If you can think of anything else, place it below.

AFTER YOUR TRIP
~Après Votre Voyage

The City of Light and Love is known for its love of the arts. Words are not everyone's favorite way to express their appreciation of the beauty that they have experienced. I have dedicated a few pages for you to use as blank canvases to sketch what you saw in Paris that left a mark on you. Your experience can be enjoyable, sad, frustrating, or awe-inspiring. Remember, this is your journal about your experience. Make it your special keepsake.

The Artist

~L'artiste

The Artist
~L'artiste

The Artist

~L'artiste

The Artist

~L'artiste

The Artist
~L'artiste

The Artist

~L'artiste

The Artist

~L'artiste

The Artist
~L'artiste

The Artist

~L'artiste

The Artist
~L'artiste

The Artist

~L'artiste

The Writer
~L'écrivain

Did you speak French on your trip?

_____

_____

_____

_____

_____

Were you able to find the obelisk from The Princess of Sapphires and Sand? *It is located in the Place de la Concorde in **the eighth arrondissement** of Paris, France.*

_____

_____

_____

_____

_____

_____

_____

_____

Which museums did you visit?

_____

_____

_____

_____

_____

_____

Who was your favorite artist?

_____

_____

_____

_____

_____

_____

Which was your favorite piece of art? Why?

_____

_____

_____

_____

_____

_____

Did you see any famous sculptures? Think about it. Were you able to find Rodin's "The Thinker"? He is always waiting to have a conversation with you in arrondissement seven.

_____

_____

_____

_____

_____

Did you try all of the food on your list?

_____

_____

_____

_____

_____

Which were your favorite arrondissements?

_____

_____

_____

_____

_____

Did you ride the Metro? If so, did you enjoy it?

_____

_____

_____

_____

_____

_____

Did you do a Seine River Cruise?

_____

_____

_____

_____

_____

Did you see the hunchback of
Notre-Dame or the gargoyles?

_____

_____

_____

_____

_____

_____

Did you visit the Eiffel Tower?
Did you take the stairs or the elevator?

Which souvenirs did you bring home?

Safe travels, and happy reading!

www.ingramcontent.com/pod-product-compliance
Lightning Source LLC
Chambersburg PA
CBHW051644120626
46551CB00015B/2209